ENTERING THE REALMS OF GOD'S LOVE: 7 KEYS TO FALLING IN LOVE WITH JESUS

INSPIRED AND REVEALED BY THE HOLY SPIRIT

WRITTEN BY

SHAWDAE RENEE

Copyright © 2023

DEDICATION

This book is dedicated to the Love of my Life, the Life of my love, Jesus Christ. Whom I encountered at the tender age of 18 and never looked back.

TABLE OF CONTENTS

Introduction - 3

Self-Reflection - 6

Chapter One

The Main Key: Your soul must be knit to Jesus - 8

Chapter Two

Embrace communication and love

Language of Jesus - 11

Chapter Three

Engage Your Senses and Imagination:

See In The Spirit - 16

Chapter Four

Have Faith and Believe that God is... - 22

Chapter Five

Know Him! Love Letters from God's Word - 27

Chapter Six

Meditate on the Character and Nature - 33

of Jesus Daily

Chapter Seven

Acknowledge Jesus and Desire, Jesus - 37

Bonus: 7-Day Prayer Devotional Journal - 41

INTRODUCTION

Do you ever feel stressed out, overwhelmed, and overworked? Distracted by the cares of life, you barely get to spend time with those most important to you! You may find yourself spending time with people but mentally present. Well, this is the day-to-day story of many men and women worldwide. I know a story of a young woman who struggled to balance her home, work, and spiritual life, let alone her love life. She felt tired and fed up with going through the motions of her daily routines and barely seeing the positive results she longed for, especially in her spiritual life. She grew up and served faithfully in the church, but when her world seemed dry, stagnate, and unproductive, she secretly harbored questions and thoughts, such as "Why am I a Christian? Why do I fast and study the Bible?" One day, in her little 400 square ft studio apartment, she prayed to God for a personal encounter and changed life.

With her eyes closed and heart opened, she felt the hot presence of God pour over her body. She fell into what seemed like a trance or vision as she called on Jesus with all her heart and soul. She saw a figure full of bright light, and at that moment, she heard scriptures reminding her of God's love flooding her heart and mind, washing away the uncertainty and answering lingering questions. At that moment, she heard a voice say, "You must enter the realms of my love." Some three-dimensional, glowing archway entrance appeared before her. She shook and trembled under the power of

God. The love, peace, and security she felt at the moment were almost indescribable!

One may ask, "What happened that day?" the Holy Spirit spiritually transported the young lady into a supernatural experience of a lifetime. She was in "the realms of God's love," and Jesus was at the center. What is a realm? It's a place called there! Somewhere in the supernatural but an entrance, gate, portal, or opening. Did you know that there are evil realms and godly realms? In this case, the domains we want to access lead to God's presence. She never remained the same from that day on. Through Jesus Christ, God filled the void that had kept her overwhelmed, struggling, tired, and stagnating. All her previous cares and worries seemed small now that she had found her true love, Jesus! She let Him into her heart and then communed with Him daily from that time on. Jesus finally became real and tangible to her.

Many people have heard about encounters with Jesus or have had their encounters with God, and even have accepted Christ into their hearts but lack the continual day-to-day fellowship and communion with Him. A relationship with Jesus, The Holy Spirit, and God the Father is necessary for Christians. Many take the first step of confessing Jesus as their savior but struggle with accepting HIM as LORD. Often people pray or read the Bible with little connection to Jesus, God, or the Holy Spirit. They may slowly fall into the motions or even fall away, never quite fulfilled in their relationship with God.

A relationship with Him is primarily based on your love for him and His love for you. But what's love got to do with it, you may ask? Studies have shown that most people ascribe much value to love and relationships. People are searching and longing to be loved and to love. Yet the things of this world, situations, and circumstances have caused the hearts of men to grow cold, even towards Jesus, Holy Spirit, and God. In some households, He has become a superhero or character from a book we pay homage to at certain times of the year! There's no real relationship with Jesus if there is no real love for Jesus. I am thrilled that you are reading this book! Whether you are new to Christ or someone who has been in the faith for years, we can all benefit from cultivating a more profound love for and fellowship with Christ Jesus. Did you know that love is a journey? You are about to embark on a spiritual journey that will change your life forever! Imagine you're packing for a trip of a lifetime. You load your spiritual, emotional, and physical "baggage" in your vehicle and take off. Jesus is the vehicle of God's love, so falling in love with Jesus drives you straight into God's love! But before we can take off, we need our keys. That's where this book comes in, and I hope you will join me for the ride.

SELF-REFLECTION

Ask yourself these questions and write down your responses.

Before you begin this journey, reflect by asking yourself these questions.

1. Have I ever loved someone or been loved by someone? What does it feel like?
2. How do I currently love others?
3. Who is Jesus, the Holy Spirit, and God to you?
4. What voids do you feel currently in your life? (What are you lacking?)
5. What is currently filling the voids? (How are you coping?)
6. What might be hindering you from loving Christ more deeply?

_____
_____
_____
_____
_____
_____
_____
_____

What is love? Meditate on 1 Corinthians 13:1-8

I may speak in different languages, whether human or even of angels. But if I don't have love, I am only a noisy bell or a ringing cymbal. 2 I may have the gift of prophecy, I may understand all secrets and know everything there is to know, and I may have faith so great that I can move mountains. But even with all these, I am nothing if I don't have love. 3 I may give away everything I have to help others and even give my body as an offering to be burned. But I gain nothing by doing all this if I don't have love. 4 Love is patient and kind. Love is not jealous, it does not brag, and it is not proud. 5 Love is not rude, it is not selfish, and it cannot be made angry easily. Love does not remember wrongs done against it. 6 Love is never happy when others do wrong, but it is always happy with the truth. 7 Love never gives up on people. It never stops trusting, never loses hope, and never quits. 8 Love will never end. But all those gifts will come to an end—even the gift of prophecy, the gift of speaking in different kinds of languages, and the gift of knowledge.

CHAPTER ONE

SOULMATE: YOUR SOUL MUST BE KNIT TO JESUS!

Have you ever read the bible passage about Jonathan and David? **1 Samuel 18:1 reads, " And it came to pass when he had made an end of speaking unto Saul, that the soul of Jonathan was knit with the soul of David, and Jonathan loved him as his soul."**

What a powerful connection and fellowship the two must have had. How much more, Jesus and you? God wants us to spend time with Jesus; as we do this, He has access to our hearts. Don't forget about the Holy Spirit, and be intentional about spending time with the Holy Spirit talking to him because he reveals who Jesus is according to the scripture in **John 14:26**, where Jesus said, **"But the Comforter, which is the Holy Ghost, whom the Father will send in my name, he shall teach you all things, and bring all things to your remembrance, whatsoever I have said unto you."**

Let Him genuinely have your heart. Are you willing to give your heart away? After all the disappointments, frustrations, and letdowns you may have faced? Unfortunately, I experienced my soul being knitted to one guy after another as I aimlessly searched for love and companionship. I was often looking for love in all the wrong places. Until, one day, I became tired, crying out to God to break the soul ties and heal me from past hurts. In that very moment, God took my heart and broke it for what breaks His. Here is another way to put it, the heat of God's love set my cold heart on fire, and it began to melt. A new heart appeared with new emotions, new thoughts, and more. After doing this consistently for several weeks, I saw myself becoming knot with Jesus. I was so in love I almost felt like I didn't need marriage or a man!

My relationship with Jesus reached beyond the surface to a deeper place of fulfillment, the soul. Remember, your soul comprises your mind, will, and emotions! Imagine all of your soul being in tune with the Holy Spirit. Some of the best experiences happen when your soul is enlightened. Think about when you listen to music, watch a movie, find a new friend, or engage in an Intimate relationship. You feel some satisfaction that is deeper than the surface. We must move beyond the surface, i.e., the physical, and connect to Jesus on a soul level. It's supernatural yet authentic. Don't get me wrong, your human Spirit and the Holy Spirit must also align with your soul. We want to be sure that our relationship with Jesus embodies our most authentic self. How can we do this?

- Be transparent with Jesus.
- Don't hold back
- Share your deepest desire, inadequacies, insecurities
- Just be you

Remember, This is one of the most critical keys to falling in love and maintaining your love with Jesus. Time is of the essence. We must be wise with our time because the amount of time we invest in spending with Jesus determines how

to knit our souls will be with Him. The amount of time you give determines the more connected your soul and Spirit become with Jesus! Keep reading. Let's unlock the next realm!

CHAPTER TWO

EMBRACE THE COMMUNICATION AND THE LOVE LANGUAGE OF JESUS

Have you ever read the book by Gary Chapman, **5 Love Languages**? He wrote about how people express and experience love in different ways.

Studies have shown that one of the most significant conflicts in marriage is communication. Everybody is trying to voice how they want and need to be loved. Communication issues have led many married couples to adultery, arguments, and divorce. It is our job to find out how someone wants to be loved. In this beautiful relationship with Jesus, he already knows how you want to be loved, but you need to find out how He wants love from you. So, what is the love Language of Jesus? The Bible is our best guide to knowing.

* **Obedience is a Love language of Jesus**.

John 14:15,21 *"If you love me, you will keep my commandments."* Obedience is better than sacrifice. What does it mean to obey? You do what Jesus wants and put that above what you want. Why are we obeying? Simply because we love him more than ourselves. Therefore, your relationship with Jesus requires two-way engagement.

Have you heard the saying, "Actions speak louder than words"? This phrase is biblical.

The Bible tells us in **John 10:27**, **"*My sheep hear my voice*."** **Jeremiah 33:3** says, **"*Call unto me I will answer,*"** and **Matthew 12:34** ***declares, "That out of the heart, the mouth speaks."***

Think about what you are saying and what you are hearing daily. Here are some practical tips for communicating more effectively and supernaturally with Jesus!

*   **Terms of Endearment**

In your alone time and prayer time, use terms of endearment with Jesus daily. You could use many words to express your love for Jesus, but sometimes we need help. Try using words like I love you, my love, my King, Beautiful One, Savior. If you listen to most contemporary worship songs today, many lyrics embody a love language and adoration that opens our hearts to God. For example, let's analyze the lyrics of this popular song by Maverick City Music. The song title is **"Most Beautiful ."** The title tells us an aspect of Jesus to encounter, His beauty. Why would someone call Jesus a beautiful one? The expression of love towards Jesus comes out as those two words because the songwriter may have remembered the perfectly pure savior we have in Jesus. The lyrics begin with

- We're in love with you
- No one else can take your place
- One thing I desire
- Only this I seek
- to dwell dwell dwell

- Here Forever
- This will be my posture
- Laying at Your feet
- Oh, to dwell dwell dwell
- Here Forever
- Dearest Father
- Closest Friend
- Most Beautiful

These lyrics express a love language that connects heaven and the heart. This should be our daily speech to Jesus; we are communing with Him and the Holy Spirit. Go to youtube, play some of these worship songs, and meditate on the lyrics; say or sing the lyrics to the Lord Jesus with all your heart. Remember, God is love!

*   **Crazy Faith**

I know this may feel or sound crazy at first, but it works! Think about what comes from your heart when you think about Jesus, what he's done for you, and who he is. Find the expression of that through words. You may need to look it up in the dictionary or use similar words we see in scripture as the disciples praise God. Whatever you do, step out of your comfort zone! Jesus is honest, but He will be no more natural to you unless your FAITH makes Him real. Stepping out of the box, in this case, takes FAITH! **Hebrews 11:3 "Through faith we understand that the worlds were framed by the word of God so that things which are** *seen were not made of things which do appear ."* **Hebrews 11:6** *"But without faith it is impossible to please him: for he that cometh to God must believe that he is and that he is a rewarder of them that diligently seek him ."* **John 11:40** *"Then Jesus said, "Did I not tell you that if you believe, you will see the glory of God?"*

* **Tone and Intentions**

Communicate lovingly with loving words in general. Remember, the Bible says to love others as you love yourself. So people can somewhat judge how you love God based on your love for others! Wow, that's heavy! Your intentions Influence a response to Jesus. We live in a society today where people look to Jesus for things they want or what they can get out of him. Give me, give me, give me. My name is Jimmy. People often get what they need from God and go after the next lust or desire. It's OK to desire things from God, but Jesus wants a sincere heart according to **Psalm 51:17**, *"A broken and a contrite heart, O God, thou wilt not despise,"* and **Matthew 5:8**, *"Blessed are the pure in heart, and they shall see God."*

* **Topic of Discussion and Conversation**

Try talking to Jesus about any and everything! Believe that He is there with you as the Bible says, and hold conversations with Him. Wait for a response, make sure the answer is not contrary to the Bible, write down what He says, and meditate on it! Remember, sometimes God speaks with visuals, thoughts, flashes of pictures, etc., so be open to how God speaks to you. The fact that God has a particularly unique way that he wants to talk to you is a testament to his love for you.

* **Know Who You Are With**

Know His word and what it says about you! The best love stories and relationships consist of partners knowing each other's thoughts toward them. The Bible is the most significant source, along with the Holy Spirit, to help us understand what Jesus thinks of us and know who Jesus is. Knowing someone's character influences your vulnerability to be open and authentic with them. Find scriptures that speak to the nature of Christ and meditate on them. For example, in **Matthew 9:36,** Jesus is Compassionate; **in John 3:16,** Jesus is Loving; and **in Luke 23:34,** Jesus is forgiving.

CHAPTER THREE

IMAGINE YOURSELF WITH JESUS!

Have you ever tried to spend time with Jesus, and it feels weird, dry, or silent? Unfortunately, studies show that a high percentage of Christians spend very little time in prayer with God, on an average of about 5 minutes daily. Why? Wouldn't you become distant if you constantly leave your prayer-time feeling like nothing has changed or unfulfilled with unresolved issues? Perhaps this could be why so many people are quick to do something other than spend time with God. You may need to change your approach to God and prayer. Listen, God has given us eyes to see! Vision is one of the most potent tools to spend time with Jesus.

The Bible says in **Psalm 119:18, "Open my eyes, that I may behold wondrous things out of your law." Matthew 5:8 "Blessed are the pure in heart, for they shall see God."** Imagine you're in a relationship with someone but never really see or hear from them. You would struggle with trust and security, eventually drifting away to other things that seem more real. If we are in a relationship with Jesus, we should see Him. According to the Bible, we can see Him in various ways, such as light and word. **John 8:12 "When Jesus spoke again to the people, he said, "I am the light of the world. Whoever follows me will never walk in darkness but have the light of life." John 1:1 "In the beginning was the Word, and the Word was with God, and the Word was God."** We also know He was a man here on earth and is described as a male in the Bible. We don't know what Jesus looks like, but the Bible gives us context that helps us correctly see Jesus. Jesus reveals Himself to us in many ways. The Bible is the key to understanding whether what you see is from God. What you see should confirm the character of Jesus as stated in the holy scriptures. Remember, the Holy Spirit is here to help us see Jesus, so rely on the Holy Spirit to help you see Jesus.

The devil knows how powerful seeing is, and that is why the Bible says in
John 12:40 "He has blinded their eyes and hardened their heart, lest they see with their eyes, and understand with their heart, and turn, and I would heal them." We see with our spiritual eyes and gain understanding in our hearts.
Jesus desires for you to interact with Him and see how he sees. According to **John 17:24, "Father, I want those you had given me to be with me where I am and to see my glory, the glory you had given me because you loved me before the creation of the world"** Jesus prayed that we would see the glory and more. When we use our spiritual eyes, we encounter God's glory, which is given because God loves us. This is why we have learned that the realms of God's love are a place, and God wants us in Him.

Look at this scripture in **1 John 4:16 "And we have known and believed the love that God hath to us. God is love, and he that dwelleth in love dwelleth in God and God in him."** We need to dwell in the presence of God. Do you see the disadvantages of spending little time with God? There is power in dwelling with Jesus, taking time to sit, talk, and fellowship with Him. When you do this, you are in the realms of GOD'S LOVE. God's love is a place, and Jesus is the entry point. The Holy Spirit will help you to get to Jesus, and Jesus will help you get to God. Jesus even says in **John 10:27, "My sheep hear my voice." 1 John 16:13 "When the Spirit of truth comes, he will guide you into all the truth, for he will not speak on his authority, but whatever he hears he will speak, and he will declare to you the things that are to come."** God gave you a tool you were born with to further assist you in seeing. God gave you an imagination! Look at what **1 Chronicles 29:18** says about imagination:

"O LORD God of Abraham, Isaac, and of Israel, our fathers, keep this forever in the imagination of the thoughts of the heart of thy people, and prepare their heart unto thee." According to this Scripture, God uses imagination to help you remember. Remember what? The word of God, the ways of God.

Let's practice using our spiritual sight with our God-given imagination.

- First, close your eyes and quiet your environment. If you prefer, play a soft worship instrumental in the background. Next, find scripture to meditate on. It could be a scripture related to something you are praying about. Another way is to choose scriptures on issues you're facing. Now Imagine each detail in that scripture and Jesus in that scripture. You can imagine Jesus helping you with that issue or circumstance. For example, imagine yourself in the arms of Jesus and write down what it feels like. You should feel a sense of warmth, protection, and connection. You may also feel love, belonging, and security. Imagine yourself holding the hand of Jesus, hugging Him, eating with Him, laughing with Him, and even when you sleep lying with Him.

Do life with Jesus! See yourself singing and dancing with Him in the spiritual and the physical. This practice allows our alone time with Jesus to become more meaningful and engaging. Jesus can fill every void in our lives as we practice seeing with our spirit. Let's say you have been praying about healing for your body, meditating on **Isaiah 53:5** says, **"But He was wounded for our transgressions, He was bruised for our iniquities; the chastisement for our peace was upon Him, And by His stripes, we are healed."** You can imagine the stripes on his back, the sickness you're dealing with given to Jesus, Jesus taking the illness from you, and Jesus touching you. Wait a bit and write down what else you see or hear, as Jesus will expound upon scripture or direct you in the way He wants. Practice doing these things daily. Make sure you spend quality time with Him throughout your day to get the most from God.

In your alone time with Jesus, do not forget to write down visuals that flash before your eyes and ensure nothing contradicts the Bible. Keep a record of your experiences and encounters to refer to in the future when needed. This will encourage you and help you see the mighty ways God has revealed himself to you as you have grown in your relationship with Jesus.

REAL-LIFE EXAMPLE

A very educated lady held a full-time job and was deeply invested in ministry work. She had a whole load of things to do day to day! However, when it came to her daily walk with Jesus, she was all in! She imagined holding Jesus' hand while walking down the street, giving her peace and protection! On her lunch breaks, she imagined Jesus sitting at the table with her, which resulted in her listening to Him more and receiving divine revelations. Sometimes she would see flashes of angels or flashes of words to comfort her. One day while eating with Jesus, she began to tell him about some of her struggles in life, and all of a sudden, she got quiet and heard a still, small voice tell her a book of the Bible, chapter and verse! She looked it up, and it addressed the exact area the woman was talking to Jesus about!!!

No one can deny that she was there with Jesus, and he spoke back to her during her lunch date by the power of the Holy Spirit! She experienced continued divine revelation all because she entered the realms of God's love using God-given vision!

CHAPTER FOUR

HAVE FAITH AND BELIEVE THAT HE IS...

Did you know Jesus is always with us, especially when we pray? He is there even though you may not see or feel him physically, but He is there! How do I know? Jesus says in **Matthew 28:20,** *"And lo, I am with you always, even unto the end of the world."* **Amen.** Do you believe this scripture? If so, you should be in awe of the privilege of accessing God and His many blessings from heaven.

Christians have access to Jesus; however, deeper intimacy requires faith. "The scripture says in **Hebrews 11:6, *"Without faith, it is impossible to please God."*** Check your faith level because this key will make or break your relationship with Jesus. Imagine being in a relationship with someone, but you don't believe what they say or who they are. That relationship wouldn't last, becoming a breeding ground for mistrust, insecurity, and divorce!

The Bible tells us to **"walk by faith and not by sight! Walk by faith not by sight"** according to **2 Corinthians 5:7**. Let me remind you that In this relationship with Jesus, we must **believe that He is a rewarder of those that diligently seek Him (Hebrews 11:6).** The time you spend with Jesus is so valuable however you will get out what you put into it. Put your faith in

Jesus and His word. You will see yourself not wanting to leave His presence and diligently seeking His counsel. Faith is the key!

Humans and Christians will only have some of the answers to life's issues. Furthermore, we may need an explanation for everything happening worldwide. However, we have faith! Faith in what? Jesus and His word! Liken your faith to money or a ticket to obtain something or get somewhere. Remember, Jesus was God on earth in human form! I know by faith when I read the amplified version of **Philippians 2:7**. It reads,**"But emptied Himself (without renouncing or diminishing His deity, but only temporarily giving up the outward expression of divine equality and His rightful dignity) by assuming the form of a born-servant, and being made in the likeness of men (He became wholly human but was without sin, being fully God and fully man)."** Faith can sometimes be a mystery, but faith in God will never fail!

Let's remind ourselves what faith is. In the scripture, **Hebrews 11:1-2** Says, *"Now faith is confidence in what we hope for and assurance about what we do not see. This is what the ancients were commended for."* To believe, to hope, and to trust despite what we see.

Again, how would you feel if you were in a relationship with a significant other and they were constantly doubting if you love them, doubting the promises you have made to them? How would you feel? Jesus wants us to believe His word and promises daily as we pray and seek Him!

- Write down a list of things you believe God for
- Find scriptures you can pair with prayer points and things you believe in God for!

I experienced this when I started to believe Jesus was in my room with me when I prayed. My devotion time remained unchanged, but it became more engaging. I became more personal and open to Jesus because I believed. I believed that Jesus was walking or driving with me, causing me to feel such peace and security. Believing caused my whole relationship with Jesus to change. Another result is that I became more authentic and discovered my true identity in Christ Jesus.

All because of Faith! I began to see miracles, breakthroughs, and deliverance in areas of my life that I could not fix with my might!

It is essential to remember that when you have faith, your actions will line up with it! **"Faith without works is dead,"** according to **James 2:20.** Your actions must follow up with what you believe. You can't say one thing and do another. For example, if you believe Jesus is with you, talk to Him. Take the step, open your lips, look at him, and speak! Believe in God's word and what He says about you. Something is so attractive about a person who is full of faith. Faith is contagious and can draw people to God.

Make sure you get rid of doubt daily! Jesus is your husband and your Maker, and that's the final why because the Bible says so! Have you ever heard the saying, "If you believe, you shall receive?" This is very true when entering the realms of God's love. Remember, it's a place in God, and faith helps you access it. Sadly, people worldwide seek fulfillment and joy by toiling to no end. Your life doesn't have to be this way!

Believing in God's love produces fulfillment, joy, and much more! When you believe, you will see!

REAL-LIFE EXAMPLE:

There was an educator who dedicated all their time and energy to their profession. They spent hours planning lessons, professional development courses, and even spending $1000 of dollars investing in materials for students. To no avail, this teacher struggled with constant behavior issues, volatile parents, and systematic barriers, causing the job they so loved to become a burden. Finally, at a breaking point, this educator cries out to Jesus. Gradually through the weeks, they fell in love with Jesus, believing He was there hearing every word. The educator started applying faith to this job situation using scriptures that combat the different areas of struggle. The teacher began to speak the word of Jesus over the classroom daily and began to imagine Jesus in the classroom with the students and staff! When unfavorable situations happen, this educator would immediately talk to Jesus about it as if he was right there. Divine solutions from the Holy Spirit began to pour out, and this educator saw a complete *turnaround in the classroom. Supernaturally, student behavior improved, parents began to comply, and academically students began to progress!*

At times, the educator felt an unexplainable peace, as well as the visitors entering the classroom. All because this teacher entered the realms of God's love by faith!

CHAPTER FIVE

KNOW HIS WORD: LOVE LETTERS FROM JESUS

Now that we have faith and can use the imagination God gave us, we can experience the reality of God's word! You know God's Word is His bond! Words are powerful. Have you ever said something jokingly, and then, to your surprise, it happened? God has created words to accomplish, carry out, and perform! How are you using your words? Are you keeping your words in line with the word? The word is the Bible and the spoken word God has given you.

The Bible says in **Philippians 4:10**, *"That I may know Him, and the power of His resurrection."* How will you know Jesus, you might ask? Through His Word! Remember, Jesus is the word according to **John 1:1**, which says, *"In the beginning was the Word, and the Word was with God, and the Word was God."* God has breathed the Holy Scriptures to help us know God, see God, and be like Christ!

The word of God is living and active according to **Hebrews 4:12.** Therefore, this Bible is a living document of living letters from God. He wants us to see beyond the letters on each page and see the Spirit behind the words. This will help us to know Jesus better! This will help us discern whether we hear from Jesus or the evil one. Remember, the Holy Spirit helps us to understand the scriptures.

Think about it this way, in marital relationships; you want to know each other's most profound thoughts, desires, and heart. Well, out of the heart, the mouth speaks! What does the mouth speak? Words!

We can see the intent, desire, and will of Jesus through God's word. Let's look at some examples in God's word now.

- Jesus shows us his intent towards us in scripture in the latter part of **John 10:10** *"I have come that they may have life and that they may have it more abundantly ."* God shows us His intent for us, and Jesus shows us his passion and love for us in **Romans 5:8,** *"But God shows his love for us in that while we were still sinners, Christ died for us."* **John 3:16** *"For God so loved the world that he gave his one and only Son, that whoever believes in him shall not perish but have eternal life."* Jesus lived out His passion and love by obeying God through dying on the cross for our sins.

- God shows us His will and desires in **Jeremiah 29:11** *"For I know the thoughts that I think toward you, says the LORD, thoughts of peace and not of evil, to give you a future and a hope."* Also, in **John 3:36,** *"Whoever believes in the Son has eternal life."* The Bible says that Jesus wants us to believe and have eternal life with God the Father. It is the will of Jesus that we are healed, accessible, and prosperous; however, we have a choice. We have free will, and Jesus doesn't impede our will or force Himself on us. He wants us to choose Him.

Knowing the word of God will transform your intimacy and love for Jesus! Knowing Jesus draws a genuine response from you. Believe it or not, many people have a dysfunctional relationship with Jesus because of trust and identity issues. However, knowing who you are in Christ will help destroy identity and trust issues. These types of problems affect intimacy in relationships. What is intimacy? According to Webster's Dictionary, Intimacy is personal, private, closeness, or sexual intercourse. Imagine you marry someone who never wants to consummate the marriage or who doesn't know how to make you feel close and secure. How close are you to Jesus? What could you do to make your relationship with Him more personal? It's important to know that a relationship with Jesus requires intimacy. Find scriptures about Jesus to meditate on and study more about Jesus. The books of Matthew, Mark, Luke, and John are books all about the life and character of Jesus. Get to know Him through Word and personal prayer time. The Bible is full of powerful revelations and knowledge concerning Jesus.

A beautiful woman in her thirties was serving the Lord and was very successful in her career. But whenever people saw her, they would ask her why she was unmarried. She had been waiting for God to bring her the right person, but it seemed no one had been a good fit. She began to feel periods of loneliness and, at times, frustration because she felt delayed. She battled comparisons when others would get married or have kids before her.

Consequently, this drove her closer to Jesus. She once heard someone say Jesus is your husband. This comment was weird and perplexing to her, but she decided to search the scriptures. In **Isaiah 54:5** it says," **For thy Maker is thine husband; the LORD of hosts is his name; and thy Redeemer the Holy One of Israel."** This lady began to see Jesus in a different light. She also often prayed that God would help her to know who she was in Christ's eyes. She began to meditate on scriptures that affirm who she is in Christ.

Jesus revealed that she was fearfully, wonderfully made, and not forgotten. She learned that Jesus is a redeemer of time and that He is right there to guide her every step in this single season. What does God's word say about a loving Jesus as a husband?

- **Song of Solomon 2:16** I am my beloved, and my beloved is mine.

- **Song of Solomon 3:4** I have found the one whom my soul loves.

- **Isaiah 54:5** For your Maker is your husband, the LORD of hosts is his name; and the Holy One of Israel is your Redeemer, the God of the whole earth he is called.

- **Jeremiah 3:14** Turn, O backsliding children, saith the Lord; for I am married unto you: and I will take you one of a city, and two of a family, and I will bring you to Zion:

- **Ephesians 5:25-33** Husbands love your wives, as Christ loved the church and gave himself up for her, that he might sanctify her, having cleansed her by the washing of water with the word, so that he might present the church to himself in splendor, without spot or wrinkle or any such thing, that she might be holy and without blemish. In the same way, husbands should love their wives as their bodies. He who loves his wife loves himself. No one ever hated his flesh but nourished and cherished it, just as Christ did for the church.

- **Ecclesiastes 4:9** Two are better than one because they have a good return for their labor: If either falls, one can help the other up. But pity anyone who falls and has no one to help them up. Also, if two lie down together, they will keep warm. But how can one keep warm alone?

Many people have said the sinner's prayer, but have you accepted Jesus as Lord over your life? Lord is another word for king, ruler, or even husband! Research shows striking similarities among these roles, such as the need to submit and embrace authority. Now that we know Jesus is our Lord and husband, amongst many other functions, we can fully immerse ourselves in true intimacy with

Him. Remember, knowledge is vital to unlocking the realms of God's love!

CHAPTER SIX

MEDITATE ON THE CHARACTER/ NATURE OF JESUS DAILY

A character says a lot about a person. I'm sure you've heard of the phrase **"The apple doesn't fall far from the tree"** or the scripture in **Matthew 7:20 "You shall know them by their fruits."** Well, how do we know Jesus? We know Him by His fruits! Fruits are synonymous with the character. Sadly, many relationships today are based on material things instead of character development. Often, people need more vetting to jump into relationships and new friendships. A person's character speaks louder than what you see on the outside. Now that you know Jesus is your husband and you are married to Him (spiritually speaking), you can delve further into the character of Jesus. This will help you enter the realms of God's Love. In this relationship with Jesus, you must know your partner. But guess what? The enemy hates this union between you and Jesus! Therefore, you must know the nature and character of Jesus while operating in discernment!

The HOLY SPIRIT is here to help, lead, and guide you as you continue to know Jesus. However, **"the devil comes to steal, kill, and destroy,"** according to **John 10:10.** When you spend alone time with Jesus, you have to line up what you see and hear with the character of Jesus. If it doesn't align with Jesus, it's most likely the devil. The devil is a liar and the father of all lies. He cannot be trusted, as the Bible says in **John 8:44.**

The Bible shows us the picture of a good husband. Let's match up the attributes of a good husband with Jesus for further examination. When you think of a good husband, one would say:

- **Protector:** **Psalms 18:2** The Lord is my protector; he is my strong fortress. My God is my protection, and with him, I am safe. He protects me like a shield, defends, and keeps me safe. **John 17:12** During my time here, I protected [my disciples) by the power of the name you gave me.

- **Leader:** **John 13:13** Ye call me Master and Lord: and ye say well; for so I am.

- **Provider:** **Philippians 4:19** And my God will supply every need of yours according to his riches in glory in Christ Jesus. **Matthew 21:22** whatever you ask in prayer, you will receive if you have faith.

- **Builder:** **Hebrews 3:3** Jesus has been found worthy of greater honor than Moses, just as the builder of a house has greater honor than the house itself.

- **Healer:** **Matthew 14:14** When He went ashore, He saw a large crowd and felt compassion for them and healed their sick.

The Bible also references many stories that display the beautiful attributes of Jesus:

- The woman who was about to be stoned experienced Jesus as a protector!

- The woman at the well-experienced Jesus was someone she could talk to who would listen and be merciful towards her.

- The women with blood issues experienced Jesus as a healer, comforter, and provider as He provided the healing she longed for.

- Mary and Martha experienced the leadership of Jesus as they followed him as disciples day after day.

The character of Jesus speaks for itself.

Wow, what a privilege and honor to be in union with such a Man!

- Remember, Jesus is gentle, kind, patient, loving, thoughtful, generous, giving, and more. Study the Bible daily to find out more about the character of Jesus. We can use scriptures and biblical scenes to remind us of His character and nature.

- Remember, Jesus is holy, faithful, forgiving, loving, and compassionate! You can easily discern and dispel them if negative thoughts or contradictory words come about Christ's character. Remember to use the scriptures you have accumulated and the knowledge you gained about your husband, Jesus! His love is for you, and no devil or lying voice of the enemy can ever change that.

Real-life example:

I knew a woman who spent many years trying to live for God. She would go to church, serve in the church, and give financially, as most Christians do. However, she would often go through seasons of anxiety, worry, and fear, causing her sometimes to withdraw and put on a façade around others. Sometimes she would feel like she wasn't good enough despite everything she did for God. She often experienced much rejection, and the enemy used this as a stronghold throughout her life. Until one day, she listened to a message and began to get revelations about her identity in Christ and who Christ is. This young lady realized that she had a tainted view of Christ. She would often clump Jesus in the categories of all the men she had trauma and pain with. The scripture showed her the contrary. **Isaiah 54:5-8 "For thy Maker is thine husband; the Lord of hosts is his name; and thy Redeemer the Holy One of Israel; The God of the whole earth shall he be called."** *She saw how she had been redeemed from her past and realized that fear, anxiety, or inadequacy have to cease where Christ is. In the same chapter of* **Isaiah 54, verse 6** *reads,* **"For the Lord hath called thee as a woman forsaken and grieved in spirit, and a wife of youth, when thou wast refused, saith thy God."** *She realized that Jesus accepted her and that He is pleased when she trusts Him! His character drew her to true freedom in God, giving her divine access into the realms of God's love.*

CHAPTER SEVEN

ACKNOWLEDGE HIM/DESIRE HIM

Let's think about relationships, marriages, and friendships! How would you feel if the person accompanying you wherever you go never acknowledged you? How would you feel if they never acknowledged you around others or if they paid very little attention to you? Jesus deserves your time and attention! Did you know that His time and attention are on you daily according to **Psalm 121:3-4** *"He will not suffer thy foot to be moved: he that keepeth thee will not slumber. For Behold, he that keepeth Israel shall neither slumber nor sleep."* The Bible reads in **Proverbs 3:6**, *"In all your ways acknowledge Him, And He shall direct your paths."*

Psalm 37:4 says, *"Take delight in the LORD, and he will give you the desires of your heart"*! When we read **Matthew 6:21**, *"For where your treasure is there your heart will be."* We can see that we have a choice! Do we treasure the things of this world or the things of God? Whatever we treasure, that is what we desire and acknowledge. When a husband treasures his wife, he will honor her around others and celebrate her despite her imperfections. Christ is not looking for perfection but for acknowledgment. Acknowledge that you need Him, He is Lord, and His will is better than yours.

Look at biblical examples of acknowledging and desiring the Lord displayed by avid Samuel, Jeremiah, and Job. "The Lord has heard my request for mercy. The Lord has accepted my prayer."

Psalms 6:9 "Samuel did not yet know the Lord because the Lord had not spoken directly to him before."

1 Samuel 3:7 "But those who trust the Lord will be blessed. They know that the Lord will do what he says."

Jeremiah 17:7 "Later David asked the Lord for advice. David said, "Should I take control of any of the cities of Judah?" The Lord said to David, "Yes." David asked, "Where should I go?" The Lord answered, "To Hebron.""

2 Samuel 2:1 "Everyone knows that the Lord made these things."

Job 12:9 "Who among all these does not know
That the hand of the Lord has done this."

Practical and Spiritual Ways to Acknowledge and Desire the Lord:

- Spending quality time with Him
- Prayer
- Praise and Thanksgiving
- Testifying
- Evangelizing
- Studying the word

REAL-LIFE EXAMPLE:

As a gospel minister, I honor my Lord's Savior publicly before teaching or preaching. I give thanks and praise to Him publicly. Remember, natural husbands, want to be respected and honored. Why not do that and more for the one who gave His very life for you? As a worship leader, I have noticed the atmosphere changes when I sing worship and praise songs. Why? Because praise and worship acknowledge Jesus directly. Genuine praise and worship take your mind off of yourself and others, shifting the focus on God, Jesus, and the Holy Spirit. Whenever I'm studying the word or praying, I acknowledge out loud and in my heart that Jesus is with me, and I desire to know Him more!

SUMMARY

What a beautiful journey you can have with Jesus. I hope you have gained insight into how your relationship with Jesus can become more real, authentic, and profound. Remember, there are so many ways that God reveals Himself to us, and the keys mentioned in this book are just a few keys that help jumpstart your access into the realms of God's love. Life is a journey, and we need Jesus, with the help of the Holy Spirit, to get to our kingdom destination. God's love will sustain us and drive us through every obstacle and situation life throws at us as long as we keep our eyes on Jesus. God Bless you, and I invite you to partake in the 7-day prayer journal attached to this book.

Share your testimony about how this book has impacted your life, and write to us at shawdaerenee@gmail.com or @ShawdaeRenee via Facebook, Instagram, and all other social media platforms.

BONUS: 7-Day Prayer Journal

Each day is prophetic and divinely chosen for you to encounter Jesus in the fullness of His love and mercy! Use each day of the devotional to pray for seven days and then repeat, starting the 7-days over again each week! Watch your prayer life and relationship with Jesus intensify and take off to another level. Enter the realms of God's love now!

Day 1: Enter In

Ephesians 3:12 In him and through faith in him we may approach God with freedom and confidence.

Hebrews 4:16 Let us, therefore, come boldly unto the throne of grace, that we may obtain mercy, and find grace to help in time of need.

Lamentations 3:22-23
It is of the Lord's mercies that we are not consumed because his compassions fail not.23 They are new every morning: great is thy faithfulness.

- Write down what God is speaking and revealing to you through these scriptures. In this season of life, what is God showing you?
- Pray that God will help you to "ENTER IN"!
- Plead for mercy, plead the blood of Jesus, and let God wash clean from every sin, past mistake, failure, lying voice, etc.

_____
_____
_____
_____
_____
_____
_____
_____
_____
_____
_____
_____
_____
_____

Day 2: Jesus, I believe!

Hebrews 11:6 ESV
And without faith, it is impossible to please him, for whoever would draw near to God must believe that he exists and that he rewards those who seek him.

Romans 10:17 ESV
So faith comes from hearing and hearing through the word of Christ.
- Pray that God will strengthen your faith and help you believe in this and all seasons of life!
- Meditate on these scriptures and believe that Jesus is with you now!
- Write down what God is speaking and revealing to you through these scriptures.
- In this season of life, what is God showing you?

_____
_____
_____
_____
_____
_____
_____
_____
_____
_____
_____
_____
_____

Day 3: Open My Eyes, Open My Ears Now!

Psalm 119:118 (NLT)
Open my eyes to see the wonderful truths in your instructions.

Job 42:5
I have heard of You by the hearing of the ear,
But now my eye sees You

Revelation 4:2 (ESV)
At once, I was in the Spirit; behold, a throne stood in heaven, with one seated on the throne.

> •Pray that God will open your eyes and ears spiritually and physically!
> •Meditate on these scriptures, close your eyes, connect your imagination with the word, quiet yourself, and write what you hear!
> •Write down what God is showing you right now! Nothing is too small or too big, or too weird! Please write it down! Then pray on it according to God's will.

Day 4: Jesus Search My Heart

Psalm 139:23-24
Search me, O God, and know my heart: Try me, and know my thoughts: And see if there be any wicked way in me, And lead me in the way everlasting.

Psalm 51:12
Restore the joy of your salvation and grant me a willing spirit to sustain me.

- Pray that Jesus will search your heart.
- Meditate on this scripture and ask God to reveal any sin, wickedness, error, etc.
- Repent and ask Jesus to forgive, cleanse, and restore you!
- Write down what Jesus is speaking and revealing to you through these scriptures.
- In this season of life, what is God showing you about your relationship with Him?

Day 5: Jesus, I Humbly Submit

James 4:7-10 (KJV)

<u>Submit yourselves, therefore, to God.</u> Resist the devil, and he will flee from you. Draw nigh to God, and he will draw nigh to you. <u>Cleanse your hands, ye sinners, and purify your hearts, ye double-minded.</u> Be afflicted, mourn, and weep: let your laughter be turned to mourning and your joy to heaviness. Humble yourselves in the sight of the Lord, and he shall lift you.

- Repent & Pray that God will clean you and help you to submit to His will in this season of your life!
- Meditate on these scriptures about God's forgiveness and His will.
- Write down what God is speaking and revealing to you through these scriptures.
- In this season of life, what is God showing you?

Day 6: Jesus, Fill My Mouth With Your Words

Exodus 4:15,16
And thou shalt speak unto him, and put words in his mouth: and I will be with thy mouth, and with his mouth, and will teach you what ye shall do.

Isaiah 51:16
And I have put my words in thy mouth, and I have covered thee in the shadow of mine hand, that I may plant the heavens, lay the foundations of the earth, and say unto Zion, Thou art my people.

- Pray that God will fill your mouth with His words.
- Meditate on scriptures about God's word.
- Write down what God is speaking and revealing to you through these scriptures.
- In this season of life, what is God showing you?

_____
_____
_____
_____
_____
_____
_____
_____
_____
_____
_____
_____

Day 7: Use Me, Lord!

2 Timothy 2:21-26 ERV
The Lord wants to use you for special purposes, so clean yourself from evil. Then you will be holy, and the Master can use you. You will be ready for any good work. Stay away from the evil things a young person like you typically wants to do.

Isaiah 43:7 KJV
Even everyone that is called by my name: for I have created him for my glory, I have formed him; yea, I have made him

Deuteronomy 6:13 GNT
Honor the Lord your God, worship only him, and make your promises in his name alone.

- Pray that God will make you a vessel of honor, useful for His glory.
- Meditate on scriptures about honoring God.
- Write down what God is speaking and revealing to you through each scripture.
- In this season of life, what is God showing you?

Made in the USA
Middletown, DE
20 July 2023